long

e

Sounds & Letters 19

T0025484

KNOWLEDGE BOOKS

meat	seat
feet	sheep
key	tree
bee	

meat

3

seat

feet

sheep

key

11

tree

13

bee

15

meat	seat
feet	sheep
key	tree
bee	

Knowledge Books and Software

PO Box 50 Sandgate, Queensland 4017 Australia
p. +617-55680288 f. +617-55680277 email: sales@kbs.com.au

First Published 2022
ISBN 9781922516916
Text and editing: Carole Crimeen
Design and layout: Suzanne Fletcher
Publisher: Robert Watts

Series Information: **Sounds and Letters**

Credits

Photographs: Cover © wee dezign; p. 1 © Black-Photogaphy, Good luck images, Marcos Mesa Sam Wordley, Patthana Nirangkul; p. 3 © Ermak Oksana; p. 5 © xalien; p. 7 © Yavdat; p. 9 © Baronb; p. 11 © evkaz; p. 13 © Jan Martin Will; p. 15 © irin-k/Shutterstock.

Phonic support books are a wonderful resource for emergent readers as they encourage independent reading and help students make the link between letters and the sounds they represent.

Have students identify the images on the title page to listen for the long or short vowel sound that they will hear through the book.

Encourage students to point to each word as they read through the book.

ISBN: 9781922516916

9 781922 516916 >

KNOWLEDGE BOOKS

Sounds&Letters